The True Point
of Beginning

The True Point
of Beginning

A Memoir

Barbara G. Bedell

Library of Congress Control Number:		2011910994
ISBN:	Hardcover	978-1-4628-9746-9
	Softcover	978-1-4628-9745-2
	Ebook	978-1-4628-9747-6

This book was printed in the United States of America.

To order additional copies of this book, contact:
Xlibris Corporation
1-888-795-4274
www.Xlibris.com
Orders@Xlibris.com
101063

Dedication

To Janice and to Barbara and to Maureen who believed in me with gentle encouragement and wise commentary, I am deeply grateful.

To Jan and Suzi who gave without question their extraordinary generosity, I am very thankful. And to the men and women of Orcas Island Fire and Rescue, there are not words enough.

SUMMER 2007

Coming to terms with the death of a partner through letters, diaries, and journals is not unusual, and so I cannot claim an original perspective or a new viewpoint on the profound, all-encompassing sorrow such a death brings, nor can I offer any advice except the stages of my personal progression through the first five years after my husband died. My hope in writing this memoir is that a reader in a similar situation will find a chord that resonates with his or her feelings and then will discover the comfort that comes from a shared experience, from knowing that one is not alone on this most arduous of journeys toward survival, acceptance, and a new definition of self.

I find myself unable to start at the beginning—or perhaps I should say the "ending"—that April day in 2002 when my former life stopped for all time, when my husband of almost thirty years died of a heart attack, a death so sudden and so unexpected that I could not cry, could not pray, could not feel anything but shock and a growing awareness that my life would never be the same. Instead, I need to recall my life since that spring day from a perspective that is not necessarily orderly—one should be allowed freedom with the narrative as much as one should be allowed freedom to grieve in an individual manner, despite the expectations of others, well-meaning or otherwise. If I have learned anything from this experience, I now realize that there is no prescription for how to deal with death; that the so-called five stages of grief (disbelief, yearning, anger, depression, acceptance) do not occur in a predictable, linear manner; that what has so often been called a journey actually has no end—no final line written in black ink—of that chapter of one's life, a text safely put away on a shelf. I also believe that a conclusion in any sense of the word is not what I want. I have learned to have patience with myself; I have learned to know who I am; I have learned how to rebuild my life alone, but I will never let go of the memory of the man who, in the photographs taken throughout our married life, was always smiling and who always had his hand on my shoulder in a gesture, not of possession, but of love. For some aspects of our lives, no end is possible.

ONE

Winter Solstice—2005

To my dear friends,

I have just closed the door behind the last of the guests to leave my home at the conclusion of a neighborhood holiday party. As if the curtain had fallen on the final act of a comedy and the theatre no longer was filled with laughter and conversation, the rooms I walk through are oddly quiet and empty, and I decide to forego washing the dishes in lieu of writing this letter on the shortest day of the year. This night should be very cold, with no wind; a full moon; and deep, soft snow that carries the shadows of the tall evergreens. Instead, I look out my windows and see nothing but darkness because of the thick clouds that have clustered low in the sky all day. The wind is strong, and I can imagine the white caps on Spring Passage; the air is mild and filled with moisture—this is, after all, the Northwest.

On this night four years ago, Bruce and I arrived on Orcas Island off the coast of Washington State to stay for what we anticipated would be a long and leisurely retirement. As with so many events in our lives, no one could have predicted what would happen in April the following year, that I would be so unexpectedly alone. However, the intuition that brought us to Orcas in the first place never has proven wrong: the island simply "felt right." My feelings about this remarkable place have not lessened in the intervening years, and living here has enabled me to grow and to change in ways previously unimaginable.

Last month, I returned to the University of Iowa to attend a conference on non-fiction writing. The unusually mild fall weather made the campus all the more appealing and perhaps contributed to what a friend calls a "special sadness" when I looked back to the year Bruce and I met and the months in Iowa City that followed until he finished his residency in ophthalmology, and I received my undergraduate degree in English. The most tangible symbol of my feelings was the Gothic tower on the front of the main entrance to the old University

Hospital where I first came to know the man who would, one day, become my husband. I could see the four spires from the window of my hotel, illuminated at night, and reassuring in their endurance. The full enormity of what I had lost became more apparent to me during those few nights than ever before, but why did the recognition of this take so long? Although this question has no answer, and the journey I am on has no conclusion, I finally can accept that this is what the experience holds for me. Perhaps we have to return to our "beginnings" to see what deeper significance the endings might have.

And so such thoughts lead me on through the night. Soon, I will place a few more dishes in the sink, turn off all the lights except the nightlight in the hall, and slip under the covers for a few hours of sleep before the demands of the new day make themselves all too plainly felt. I will mail this letter to you and remember that friendship, kindness, and love are what sustain us all.

With blessings to you and yours,

TWO

"Perhaps we have to return to our 'beginnings'...."
November 2005

From a letter to a friend:

I am standing at the window of my hotel room in Iowa City, looking southwest as the sun is starting to set over this Midwest city so dear to my heart. The medical complex across the river is dark, yet I look for the Gothic tower (the entrance to the original hospital) and am surprised to see the four grey spires still rising above the austere modern buildings, the white parking ramps, the empty football stadium. I am relieved the tower is still visible because suddenly it is vitally important to me—a symbol, perhaps—one I had never thought about until now.

Bruce and I met in Iowa City at the height of the Vietnam War in the building with the Gothic tower: I was charting temperatures as a ward clerk earning money to support my rather vague attempt at an English major; Bruce was finishing a considerably more focused fourth-year fellowship in neuro-ophthalmology when he rapidly rounded the corner into the surgical area (he always walked as if he were late for an important meeting), smiled, and said, "Well, hello there."

Looking at the tower brought back so many memories: all that I have denied, tried to erase, tried to forget. Am I only now, after three years, finally acknowledging the magnitude of my loss, dropping the facade, the masquerade? Did my anger and my pain prevent my confronting the depth of what has happened to me . . . and what I have allowed to happen to myself over these past months?

My memories of our life together had always been clouded and compromised by recollections of the problems and difficulties attendant in our marriage, but now I realized that I could remember the good, generous, caring man who, in a fellow physician's assessment, was an "icon" in ophthalmology, but who, in the words of another friend who had recognized my husband's limitations, knew that

Bruce was a husband who "had loved [me] in the only way he could, and with as much emotion as he was capable of feeling"—an assessment that I will never completely understand because this friend, too, is now gone.

The sunset grows more deeply red as the diffuse white lines of eight jet con trails bisect the fair weather clouds that streak across the sky. Bruce always counted the jet trails, wondering where the planes were going. How he loved to travel—a restlessness in his temperament that drove him to see as much of the world as possible. One of my favorite photographs shows him at 18, standing casually and smiling at whoever was taking the picture, the Eiffel Tower tall in the background. So many images of my husband caught in the camera's eye, always laughing at me as I told him to stand still for "just one moment, please," the backgrounds running through my mind like the rivers we traveled together: the Arno, the Amazon, the Themes, the Ganges, the Luangwa, the Seine. How will I ever return to Paris, Florence, Madrid, Venice without him? Particularly the Paris he loved: the Louvre through whose galleries and rooms we wandered, always seeking the Leonardos before we left; the outdoor cafes with their colorful striped awnings on the Champs d'Elysee where we ate lunches of toasted cheese sandwiches and drank bottles of cold white wine; the Hotel Regina with its Art Nouveau elevator which carried us down to breakfasts of hot chocolate and croissants in the old stone courtyard; the bridges across which we strolled on still summer evenings, lingering halfway and looking at the dark waters flowing beneath; the green wooden stalls on the Seine where we paged through books written in languages we could barely understand; the Tour d'Argent where the splendid pate de foie gras was served on warm buttered rolls and where we watched the Gothic towers of Notre Dame grow brighter with the night-time illumination.

Now I am alone, looking at a different Gothic tower as the sun sets, the twilight slowly dissolving the view across the river. Yet, I know I will see the old tower once again as the lights gradually reveal the spires through the blackness of the night. The spires are the accumulated details of my memories, my sorrow emerging from the darkness of feelings I had suppressed for so long. Here is my grief, finally, after all this time, a grief I can now allow myself to feel. Our beginnings together not written; our ending now mine alone to recall, to put down on paper. Bruce knew that I would be the one to survive.

"How do you know this? You can't be sure."

"I know this," was his only answer.

THREE

December 2006

A friend—a poet—sends the following verse in his Christmas letter:

Relic

It comes at last to this:
the way she fits her life
to the kitchen table top,
a store of things amiss:
stale bread, a dirty knife
and cups, unopened mail,
a chipped saucer of keys,
a wallet, a fading crop
of snapshots—no avail
against lost memories.

Dust claims each other room
that drawn shades embrace,
untouched by light or broom
for months, but for a trace
through to the stairway rail
and up, rise by slow rise,
to deeper darkness where
each evening without fail
what's left of living lies
with one no longer there.

I write to my friend in response:

"Relic" affected me with its insight into a life narrowed and compromised by loss. I look at my kitchen table and acknowledge the uncomfortable truth of the first ten lines: I see a red candle half burned from a small dinner party two nights ago; two photocopies of recipes; a partially eaten bag of potato chips; a white coffee cup with the single word "Think" written on one side and filled with pens, pencils, six-inch plastic rulers; a small green leather diary; a child's wind-up orange plastic kangaroo wearing blue boxing gloves; a smooth grey stone on which is inscribed the motto "At the worst, a house unkempt cannot be as distressing as an unlived life"; a two-line telephone missing its handset; a Sierra Club calendar from last year; a stack of unpaid bills; and a set of keys to my neighbors' house— "It comes at last to this." On more than one night, I have gone to bed with the thought that "what's left of living lies/with one no longer there." This is what poetry does for me: an awareness brought by the poet through selected details of my own emerging life, a shared understanding, the realization that when I reach the end of the poem I can say, "Yes, how true."

Throughout these passing years of a single life, I have found comfort and understanding in what the great writers—Shakespeare, Edna St. Vincent Millay, Emily Dickinson, Albert Camus, C. S. Lewis—have observed about death and about grieving. While the self-help books seemed hopelessly formulaic and repetitive, the "literature of loss" helped me through some of my darkest hours, not with a "how-to" approach for dealing with death, but rather with these writers' often painful honesty and emotional insights into their own personal experiences with this most difficult of ordeals. I needed the "Yes, how true" to realize that the answers were not easy, that reactions to death were wide and varied and personal, that grieving is ultimately a private act, a private journey which may bear a similarity in the departure point, but whose conclusion (or absence thereof) is entirely an individual matter.

FOUR

July 2002

Out of some compulsion or need I have yet fully to understand, I drove five-thousand miles to Iowa and back to Washington only two and a half months after Bruce's death. Ostensibly for practical reasons (empty storage units, remove his clothes from my family's lake cottage), this trip came to mean far more to me—a challenge that I could do something, do anything, alone. So late one July afternoon, I packed the Expedition with a few clothes, an abundance of maps, my cell phone, and my small Colt .38 handgun, the latter two objects representing my deep-seated need to feel safe, to feel secure.

From my journal:

I remember waiting at the ferry landing, struggling with an almost overpowering desire to go back, to go home—telling myself I don't need to do this, I don't need to do this. Just turn the wheel and pull out of line and go home . . . go home . . . go home. Yet, I left the engine off until the ferry started to load, and once on the boat, I looked in my rear-view mirror as the red and white striped gate came down after the last car had boarded—a stroke of finality, a commitment to what I intended to do.

I don't remember the drive through central Washington and then southeast to Oregon clearly, but I do have a sense of that warm summer afternoon as the miles passed under my tires. I pulled into Hermiston, found a motel on a road that could have been anywhere in the country, one of those abysmal arterial streets that feature auto-body repair shops, fast food restaurants, gasoline stations, convenience stores with numerous variations on the spelling of "Quick Stop" —businesses with the same unhappy women behind the counters, wearing too much make-up and worn blue jeans, women whose lives were beyond my imagining.

I walked into the drab motel room, completely undistinguished by any sense of décor, the veneer of the cheap brown furniture nicked and worn, the air flat and stale. I sat on the edge of one of the double beds, and cried for a good fifteen minutes—hating my situation, hating my life, hating the realization that no one—absolutely no one—knew where I was. Finally, and with some degree of resignation and admonishment to myself to "get on with it," I dried my eyes and walked outside in the deepening twilight and brought what little I needed for the night out of the Expedition. I couldn't bear the thought of eating alone in the restaurant across from the motel as I visualized an all-too-cheerful hostess standing behind a display case filled with coconut cream pies; German chocolate cakes; large cinnamon rolls dripping with white frosting; even larger molasses, sugar, and chocolate chip cookies—temptations for the weary traveler. Instead, I ate an apple from the basket in the motel lobby, walked outside to my room in the surprisingly soft, gentle summer air, and tried to sleep, telling myself I could still turn back once first light came.

But I didn't turn back; I *couldn't* turn back: I stayed in Ogden, Utah, the second night, the motel full of families with children (was I the only person traveling alone in the world?) and drove to Denver, Colorado, the next day where I stayed with friends who had left the Midwest to retire near their grown children. My friends were very satisfied with their new lives—as if the mile-high altitude buoyed their spirits above what the flat flood plain of the Missouri River could have offered.

From my journal:

I don't envy them their contentment, but wish beyond all imagining that Bruce had lived longer. We will not grow old together. He was convinced he would die young (did he know something he refused to tell me?); I thought he would be like his grandfather Bedell who had lived well into his nineties. They looked so much alike with the same fine blonde hair and the thick mustache that came and went depending on a whim of the wearer. "What pointless thoughts," I said to myself as I looked in the mirror over the small white wicker writing desk and suddenly "saw" a long reflection of guest bedrooms to come in the future—the rooms set aside for the friend who, like some poor relative, had "lost" her husband and had come to visit (No! I did not "lose" him. He is dead, for God's sake!). This vision was so repellent that I made the first of many promises to myself: better the cold anonymity of a hotel room than these oppressive reminders of one's state in life: the single beds, the left-over furniture not suitable for other rooms in the house, the closets full of clothes and shoes seldom worn, but "just too good to throw away quite yet."

I was forced to acknowledge once again, "We will not grow old together." Not for us the retirement of these friends who rode around their gated community's streets, their bicycles adorned with tan wicker baskets attached to the front handle bars to carry baguettes and bottles of wine home for a dinner they would share. Not for us the retirement on our island where we could have walked hand-in-hand on the tree-lined gravel roads that led to home, the home that we had built together and had lived in together for just over three months before Bruce died. "Together"—the word means nothing to me now.

My friends had asked me to write down some thoughts before I left in the "Guest Journal" kept in the wicker writing desk. I read through the entries written by others—couples—who had stayed in this room and had found warmth and comfort within these four walls. I realized that I had nothing to say, nothing to express the hollowness I felt, nothing to match the glowingly optimistic thoughts of these prior inhabitants. I placed the journal back in the drawer and slowly closed it with sadness and regret, longing for the happiness and the idealistic well-being I had found in words not my own.

After leaving Colorado, I crossed Nebraska with the help of a mystery on tape, the miles interrupted by the seasonal reconstruction of Interstate 80, the temperature increasing as I moved closer to Iowa where just inside the state line, I would turn north for the final one-hundred miles of my journey. Once on the familiar two-lane roads, I noticed the often ignored beauty of the fields of corn and soy beans: the strong stalks and golden tassels of the corn, the light and dark green leaves of the beans all rippling in the wind, and the white clouds of summer forming like mounds of soft cotton against a sky pale blue from heat and humidity.

I arrived at the lake from the south, looking for that first glimpse of those deep blue waters through the gnarled burr oaks that dominated the shore line, remembering the yearly competition in childhood with my younger brother as to who would see the lake first. This time, however, the joy of childhood was erased in another painful moment of realization that Bruce would never be here with me again. And as if to deepen my sorrow, the heat was intense, the humidity a thick fog in the mornings, obscuring even the field behind my mother's cottage with only the fiery orange of the rising sun promising another day of oppressive temperatures in the high nineties.

One afternoon I stood in the downstairs bedroom closet where for decades first my great aunt and, subsequently, I had written the dates we had opened and closed the cottage and where my brother had marked the heights of his daughters each year as they grew into their teens. I read what I had written in pencil on the old vertical boards about the last summer Bruce and I were at the lake together—the summer we saw the bluebirds, the Baltimore orioles—the summer that lingered into an unusually warm fall that kept us at the lake until early November, as if to hold us there longer than we had ever stayed, as if to keep us safe from what would come the following spring. I looked at the closet walls and all the dates carved into the wood (an unlikely place for a history of my family), and I knew that I would never write anything there again.

Other than trips to the Salvation Army and the landfill to clean out the cottage of what had belonged to my husband (his summer clothing and shoes, stacks of papers from his medical practice and the office computer that we had not taken to Washington), I remember little else of how I spent the hours during that week other than I played music well into the night, aimlessly wandering through the rooms of the old cottage, the heat and humidity from the day still oppressive as whatever wind had blown during the day died with the sun. Unable to concentrate enough to read, I played the same popular songs over and over again, allowing the superficiality of the words of loss to haunt and reinforce my sorrow in a manner I realize now was filled with the sentimentality and self-pity I had so often found in the essays of my eighteen and nineteen-year-old students who fled from the brutality of the concrete into empty clichés and abstractions while trying to write about death. What they were too young to realize was what a friend in his wisdom expressed so well—that grief is in the details, that grief is "cellular" and not "full-bodied" as most believe. "Loss—genuine, grievous loss—is something we encounter not on the philosophical level but on the molecular level. This is the dreadful, inescapable fact." This was the truth I was slowly learning.

A few evenings—the more rational ones?—I sat on the end of the dock as the stars wheeled above me, the night air still warm from the heat of the day, the waves lapping softly against my feet and the white wooden posts. How many summer nights had I spent on the end of this dock since I first started coming to the lake when I was six or seven? How many summer nights had I turned to look back at the cottage, lights burning on all the floors, my grandfather and my father reading on the porch, my mother playing solitaire, my grandmother and great aunt finishing the dinner dishes—safe haven and love within those old walls?

Now I look back, the cottage almost entirely dark except for one floor lamp I had left burning on the porch so that I could find my way safely back. Every fall when Bruce and I closed the cottage for the winter, I stood in the breakfast room for a brief moment and prayed that we all would be there the following summer: prayers for my grandparents; my great aunt; my parents; my beloved elderly neighbors; our aging golden retrievers and Norwegian elkhounds—but never for one of us. The thought that either Bruce or myself would die was so far beyond my imagination that I would have found the prospect laughable. With that lingering in my mind, I slowly walked back to the cottage, the uneven boards of the dock rough on my bare feet, the sand tracked up from the beach coarse on the dry grass, the sudden smoothness of the sidewalk a welcome relief. Once in the house, I turned off the porch light and went to bed, alone for the first time in my life in this summer house, lying awake until almost dawn, ghosts filling the rooms as I tried to sleep.

FIVE

Late July 2002

I was well into my return trip home before I resumed my journal. From my hotel room in Butte, Montana, I recalled the miles I had driven from Iowa, distances both literal and emotional. I had started north from the lake well before dawn, almost reaching Interstate 90 before I realized that I had left the gun in the bedroom bureau drawer. So I returned to the lake, driving far faster than was wise on the two-lane roads in the early morning darkness, crying tears of anger and frustration over my forgetfulness, the wasted time and miles. I imagined myself talking to a highway patrol officer who might have stopped me for speeding:

"Do you know how fast you were driving?"

"Yes."

"Why the rush?"

"Because I forgot my gun."

With the Colt now safely in my possession, I headed west—the magnificent South Dakota sky filling with enormous clouds piling up higher and higher as the hours passed, their anvil-shaped tops a warning of what was to come—a severe thunderstorm that drove me off the road for the better part of thirty minutes. I was frightened by the ominous, sickly-yellow sky and the intensity of the wind as the blinding rain obscured all visibility of the Badlands, a misnomer for an area whose sandstone formations with strata of grey and pink Bruce and I had found strangely beautiful. The storm eventually passed, and I pulled back onto the interstate, steam rising from the concrete, the air now fresh and clear in the west, the dark clouds receding behind me in the east.

After leaving Rapid City, I entered Wyoming. The sky now had that remarkable clarity which often follows bad weather, the road was smooth and straight, and I found myself liking the drive: the enormous weathered wood snow fences that foretold of severe winters to come, the herds of pronghorn antelope grazing on the short grasses, the black cattle stark against the grey-green sage here in the height of summer.

That evening I pulled off the road in Sundance and remembered the evening Bruce and I had spent here on an earlier trip west. In the small cafe filled with high school students on the way to their prom, we drank beer and ate hamburgers and wondered why our waitress named Amber was not going to the dance. One boy wore a black top hat; the girls wore no coats over their long pink, yellow, and blue pastel dresses in spite of the cold weather, their self-conscious laughter filling the room. Then the women in the sad little grocery store who had noticed Bruce's red Mustang as he pulled into a parking place in front of the entrance: "Oh, we would love to take that off your hands!" Thinking back: we were so happy that night.

The following afternoon, I stopped at a large travel center for fuel. All around me were motor homes with the owners' names carved on wooden plaques bolted to the rear doors, white vacation trailers pulled by large dusty pickups and covered with stickers indicating how many states the occupants had visited, an abundance of running and screaming children of indeterminate ages, and groups of frustrated and weary adults, some of whom looked at me quizzically as I stepped out of my vehicle alone. The noise and commotion were oppressive, and I found myself wishing I had stopped at a smaller station. However, as I locked the door of the Expedition, I noticed on the ground in front of the curb three yellow-headed blackbirds. I stood in wonderment for a few moments as I recalled how Bruce and I would search for these blackbirds in the wetlands on the way to the lake on Friday nights in the summer. Red-winged blackbirds were always in abundance, but never the yellow-headed ones, and we felt that the world had smiled upon us when we saw one. And now here in the parched grass of a crowded truck stop in Wyoming were three . . . a blessing? a coincidence? I preferred to think the former as I slowly drove out of the parking lot.

To paraphrase C. S. Lewis in <u>A Grief Observed</u>, grief is a winding valley where any or every kind of bend can reveal something new. The miles of Interstate 90 were still full of memories but something now had changed: the battlefield of the Little Big Horn was empty, dusty, haunting in the gusty winds; the drive down to Yellowstone south of Livingston on the Yellowstone River strangely foreboding. I thought I recognized the mountains we had seen outside of Chico Hot Springs where we had stayed two nights, and I imagined myself driving into the Park to see the elk once more, along with the magnificent gorge of the Yellowstone River. At the last moment, however, I hesitated, pulled over to the side of the road just before the entrance to the Park, and finally turned around once I was able to focus my eyes clearly—my sorrow and my loneliness a barrier as substantial as any wall made of brick and mortar. What was the point in seeing any of this again when Bruce would not be there with me? What <u>was</u> the point of anything in my life?

As I crossed the Continental Divide, the car was buffeted by very strong winds, huge updrafts sculpturing the towering grey and white clouds. However, the magnificence of the Montana sky could not dispel the profound sadness that encompassed me as I descended into Butte. From the bleakness of yet another forgettable motel room, I realized I had come full circle from Hermiston. I could not write, or drive, the pain away, all the time wondering if I actually had proven <u>anything</u> to myself at all.

From my journal:

25 July—Butte, Montana

Left Butte before 5:00 am. Pink morning light on the mountains, steam rising from the black cattle, the condensation from their breathing. Mist and bison in the fields. The spectacular sunrise driving away the self-doubts of the night before, the remorse, the fears . . . .

Far western Montana with twenty miles to go before the border with Idaho—I saw myself alone on the road—not an unpleasant awareness—a woman with a literal destination but with no sense of an emotional one, with no sense of any conclusion to this journey or to her life, her solitude bitter-sweet. I drifted down the miles, sheltered by the sides of the tall, deep emerald mountains covered with trees so thick that I could hardly differentiate one from another.

Just east of Spokane, Washington, I turned south, heading for Moscow, Idaho, and the home of our closest Midwest friends who had chosen this place to retire because of the proximity of two universities and the Palouse.

The Palouse was like nothing I had ever seen before: the huge, virtually treeless, rolling hills lush with myriad shades of green; the brilliant yellow of the canola crop; the occasional dark, nearly black, evergreen—a land of remarkable contrasts. Then the home of my friends on top of one of those hills, Jan's colorful tell-tales blowing in the wind as we sat outside on the flagstone patio, our conversation drifting in and out of our past lives in Iowa, our present lives in the West, now diminished by the absence of one. Jan's husband would die the next year, leaving the two of us on opposite sides of the state in circumstances so similar, once again, to almost defy coincidence.

From my journal:

26 July—Moscow, Idaho

Two am: stayed up much too late, drank far too much white wine, but none of us wanted to let go of the evening, as if the moment our conversation ceased, reality would fill the emptiness, the deep sadness beneath the thin veneer of our words would surface. As long as we kept talking, we could keep at bay what we had alluded to all night but had managed to avoid: the weight of loss and death (doesn't the word "grieve" carry that connotation of heaviness?). God, I miss Bruce so much. I know I am drunk—and a great deal lost—and I wish he would be at home waiting for me with flowers and that incredible smile. I remember when he picked me up after my written exams for my Master's with a cooler in the trunk of the Oldsmobile: glasses frosted and cold from the ice and a small bottle of Chivas Regal with which to celebrate the end of that long, mentally exhausting day.

I walked outside of my friends' guest house, quietly shutting the screen door behind me, and as I looked up at the stars, I thought of what Bruce and I had seen on other nights under other skies: Halley's comet just above the horizon on the Serenghetti plains; the Southern Cross from the deck of our ship as the lush, green Marquesas grew closer in the darkness; the reflection in the waters of Lake Dal of a spectacular full moon high in the sky over the old buildings of Srinagar; the myriad number of shooting stars and meteor showers; the constellations of Ursa Major and Minor, Cassiopeia, Orion. Bruce was always far better at making sense of the night sky. When all I saw was a random mass of pinpoints of light, he could arrange these points of light into the constellations, he could find reason and order in the complexity of the universe—this same complexity in the human body that assured him there was a higher power ("All this could not have been an accident."). He gave order and structure to my life; he gave me music, that most logical, "mathematical" of the arts (Resphigi, Wagner, Shostakovitch, Smetana, Moussorsky, Tschaikowsky); he gave me a framework for my life much like the wooden bars on which I place my needlepoint canvasses—bars that keep the material straight and even and smooth. Now I fray into the future without his presence, more fragmented than I have ever been in my life.

---

29 July—Orcas Island

I cried when I reached the ferry landing and watched the red and white gate go up this time, releasing me from the self-imposed trial of those five-thousand miles—the most difficult miles I had ever driven in my life. However, the small amount of pride I was able to muster was quickly gone when I drove down my driveway and parked the car, briefly resting my forehead against the top of the steering wheel, almost in a state of disbelief that I was home. I walked down the flagstone steps, turned the key in the lock, and stopped cold in the entranceway, the air still and musty and hot from the afternoon sun. The house was quiet, too quiet, and with a sudden weariness born of fatigue and despair, I quickly unpacked the car and threw my worn clothing into the wicker basket beside the washing machine. As I carefully returned the gun to its place in the nightstand by "my" side of the bed, I realized that it had afforded me no protection after all. Nothing could have shielded me from the cruel reality of the fact that I had returned to an empty house. He wasn't there; oh, my God: he was not there.

SIX

August 2002

Gary—an Episcopalian priest, poet, scholar, and dear friend—concluded a letter he wrote to me shortly after Bruce died with the comment "Keep looking at sunsets. Maybe a sunrise or two—but I suspect that if you've seen one, you have seen them all. Sunsets, however, are another matter." Rare was the night, then, that I did not watch the sun setting in the far distance behind Vancouver Island, each sunset as different from the next as the proverbial snowflakes.

From my journal:

Sunset—this time shades of grey with clouds filling the sky, each highlighted by the sun. A wide path moves across the calm water toward me as shafts of light break through the clouds over Vancouver Island. I miss Bruce beyond my ability to fully comprehend this loss and sorrow. His birthday is Saturday; he would have been 64. He was so young . . . . The sunlight is now illuminating the underside of the clouds in three ever-widening paths. The one coming in my direction is enlarging and turning a deep pink. I search for meaning in the clouds, the light, the water, and I pray that Bruce could be "here" with me tonight.

Is this sunset providing the message that I need? A strange effect of being in a funnel going west, with the light on the bottom of the clouds and the top of the water, perhaps whispering "Come with me; come with me west with the night." West with the Night: how I always loved the title that Beryl Markham had chosen for her book. Maybe death is easy: one just slips away into another realm. I am haunted by what Bruce may have felt as he walked to the car, as I was backing up the driveway, as his heart contracted so unevenly, as I tried to breathe for him—I will never forget the emptiness in his eyes. Was it over so fast that he did not know what had happened? Did he know that I was on the ground beside him, telling him I loved him for the last time in our lives? How <u>can</u> a life be extinguished so fast? All those days, weeks, months, and years obliterated in an instant as if he had never lived at all? A man once so alive whose existence remains only in the ephemeral memories of those who knew him.

Now the surface of the water is broken into paths of grey, pink, gold—days of gold and grey; hours of gold and lead. Now the San Juan Islands are black with mists of gold between them and Vancouver Island, and a bright beam of light is moving across the water, so bright I can no longer look. A minute later and the sun is now behind the clouds; my world grows dark once again. Off to my left, San Juan Island is still green with light touching the very top of the evergreens. Two boats have headed down Spring Passage—how I would like to know where they are going, their wakes mingling together on the water like two lovers in an embrace. The back lighting is still intense but fading slowly as I watch. I do not know where I am; I do not know where I may be going; I do not know. How will I ever learn to live in those hours that life gives us that are beyond measure? How will I ever find a meaning and a purpose to life? How will I ever learn that the spiritual I seek is found in the fog that covers the valleys on early autumn mornings, in the mirror reflections of the ponds near my home, in the fiery glow of the madrona trees caught in the light of the setting sun, in the fragrance of the firs after a spring rain, in the love of my dog who waits by the door until I return, in the transcendent <u>human</u> love so eloquently stated in Psalm 139?

> *If I take the wings of the morning, and dwell in the uttermost parts of the sea; Even there shall thy hand lead me, and thy right hand shall hold me. If I say, Surely the darkness shall cover me; even the night shall be light about me.*

How will I ever learn? How will I ever know?

SEVEN

Labor Day Weekend—2002

That September, I returned to the lake to close the cottage for the winter, but this time I wisely abandoned any thoughts of driving as I boarded a flight for Minneapolis and watched the enormous, anvil-shaped thunderstorm clouds slip by my window, the fields of late summer now tan and brown and dry from a perspective of 35,000 feet.

Once at the lake, I noticed that hints of the fall and winter to come were everywhere: the leaves of the sumac bushes on the roads behind the cottage had started to turn a brilliant deep red, and the cattails in the ditches had "exploded," too late now to gather a bouquet for the vase on the front porch. Acorns from the old burr oaks covered the ground and were as slippery as marbles on the sidewalks which I dutifully swept so that no one would fall and break a leg, as my grandmother had warned me countless times when she handed the ancient broom to me, its straw irregular and thin from years of wear. The song of the cicadas filled the trees through the shorter daylight hours; the little black coots arrived, along with the Canada geese that swam past the dock every morning, stately in a manner that only large water birds such as geese and swans possess. In the afternoons, enormous flocks of blackbirds darkened the sky for minutes on end, flying to some far southern destination. I remembered the morning two or three years ago when Bruce and I sat transfixed in the boat as a large flock of white pelicans spiraled up from the lake, their black-tipped wings barely moving as the birds circled on the thermals to gain altitude while the morning sun rose higher in the sky. I remembered a time even further back when we spent a week at the Aransas National Wildlife Refuge in Texas, hoping to find the whooping cranes whose number Bruce had tracked since childhood. We searched with our guide for two days and were growing resigned to the fact that we might not see them when, on the third afternoon, four of the magnificent birds flew over our boat, much like the pelicans with their white feathers and black wingtips—a sight so special that I see the cranes now in my mind almost as clearly as I saw them then. Cranes—the birds of heaven, the birds that mate for life.

Gone were the pale skies of summer, now replaced with the deep blue of fall that only intensified the color of the lake water. The sunsets were cloudless and glowed with a red intensity that would deepen as the temperatures started to fall. Occasionally during the night, I would hear the calls of a flock of Canada geese high above me, and in the mornings, the sounds of distant shotguns broke the silence before dawn as the hunting season began. I slowly walked through my neighbors' yards along the shore, the dry leaves whirling around my feet as I noticed the dock men raising boat hoists onto the lawns. Soon the shoreline would be empty in anticipation of the winter to come when the lake would freeze and fishermen would drive their pickups onto the surface and park next to their shacks, surrounded by the intense whiteness of snow and ice.

During the late hours when I wandered through the quiet rooms unable to sleep, I now listened to Verdi and Puccini and Wagner, to Tosca, to Butterfly, to Isolde—their loss, their grief, the music and the lyrics an embodiment of the most fundamental, the most profound experiences we all face—a distillation of what it means to be human, of what it means to love deeply, of what it means to lose that love, of what it means to die, of what it means to live.

On the last day of my stay, I vacuumed the sand from the rugs; emptied the aging red refrigerator and tied its two doors open with a soft cotton dish towel; removed the remaining lawn furniture from the dock, its white paint now starting to peel from a summer's worth of wet feet (canine and human) running over the long uneven boards; covered the furniture with old sheets; and turned the waste paper baskets upside down so that the mice who moved in as soon as all human habitation had ceased would not fall into them and die from starvation.

Later that afternoon, I wrote a letter to Bruce, an "assignment" I needed to complete and had effectively postponed until this moment when I could not avoid it any longer. My therapist was a woman so gentle, so kind, and so perceptive that I viewed her more as a friend in the truest sense of the word than as a clinical psychologist with a client struggling to find herself through a labyrinth of grief and personal inadequacies. She had suggested the letter as a possible path toward greater understanding of Bruce, of myself, and of our relationship. With a sigh of resignation, I sat in front of the keyboard, my fingers tapping the letters, unable to establish just how and where to begin, feeling somewhat like a resentful student faced with writing a difficult essay.

I started with my final entry on the closet wall of almost a year ago when Bruce and I had closed the cottage together for the last time—my sorrow growing as I remembered my promise to myself that never again would I half-carve, half-write onto the thin hard old boards the dates, the weather of another cycle of spring and fall. I recalled the pair of bluebirds we saw on the lawn outside the breakfast room one morning early in May; the orange and black feathers of the Baltimore orioles as they flashed through the green leaves of summer; the female wood duck that nested in a box that we had nailed high on an old pine, her ducklings eventually tumbling to the ground below like soft balls of light grey down, the brilliant male returning to his mate only at night—the box now empty as the last two seasons of the year approached.

These thoughts were the catalyst I needed, and when I finally stopped typing, the cottage was completely dark except for the little pool of light in the corner of the living room in which I sat, the hours of that afternoon having vanished as I composed this letter to my husband. I wrote about our respective failures with each other; I wrote about the negative parts of our relationship—the anger, the destructive arguments that served no purpose, the resentments, the jealousies. However, I soon learned that this was the direction that I did not want to go. I needed to concentrate upon the positive once more as my recollections had done earlier to bring this man with whom I had lived for so long into sharper focus and with the fairness that his memory deserved.

Lake Okoboji

Labor Day weekend—September 2002

My dear Bruce,

****

Our problems and our failures aside, we had so many happy days together, including one that was perfect. Remember Lamu? Remember the Peponi Hotel and our room with the cool maroon tile floors, the mosquito nettings over the single beds, the tan and white dog that "adopted" us during our stay, sleeping on the porch every night until we awoke with first light? Remember the day we went fishing with one of those British expatriates whom one encounters all over the world—men managing somehow to survive without any visible means of support, their hair usually thinning and pale blond, their skin coarse from too much sun and far too much alcohol? We reeled in yellow-fin tuna and dorado until our arms ached; you caught a magnificent sail fish. Remember how we ate the tuna and the dorado that evening under the outdoor trellis covered with flowering vines, the lights along the white stone walls casting a soft yellow glow, the night air sweet and heavy with the softest of onshore breezes? I remember thinking at the time that I would always have this memory, this flawless day to comfort me when the bad times came.

We shared so many common interests; you introduced me to scores of classical music with which I was not familiar; we traveled to so many places, most of which I thought I would never see. You loved animals, art, antiques, birthdays, books, boating, fireworks, holidays—need I go on through the alphabet? You were a kind and compassionate man when you wanted to be; you were generous with your money and your time; you valued family and close friends so much; you considered honesty the cardinal virtue. You loved to laugh—so many people remembered your wonderful sense of humor. How I cherished the moments when you walked through the front door with your arms full of groceries and flowers and that special smile. Your patients admired and respected you as did your colleagues. How I wish you could see the many cards I received after your death. You were treasured by so many people, and I think you failed to see that at the end. I always wondered about a friend's remark that I had brought you the only happiness that you were capable of feeling. What did he know about you that I missed? There were parts of your life that you never could or would reveal to me, and I never felt safe enough to ask.

****

Why did it take me so long to realize that you never had a woman truly love you until we were married? How lonely you must have been as a child, as a young man always in your brother's shadow—Edgar the favored son. Why couldn't I stop to think more often about the emptiness, the terrible hurt in your life and what it must have done to you? Why did you despise your father so much and at the same time be the only one to care for him as he lay dying—your mother long dead from rheumatic fever when you were just five? You would have welcomed back your children from your disastrous first marriage with open arms, but they were lost to you. They never stopped to consider that there was another side to the story spun to them by their mother. Your children missed knowing a remarkable man. Likewise, I have to realize that I did not know you well at all. Did I ever try hard enough to discover you, or was I too focused on myself, too afraid to ask? I do not know what to say because I do not know.

I wish I could tell you I am sorry for so much; I wish you could tell me the same. We would erase this blackboard and start again. We are so capable of forgiveness as human beings. I hope you know this wherever you are—that you can hear my thoughts and prayers. I miss you. I miss your intelligence, your kindness, your goodness, your love. We were friends; we were strangers. We were lovers; we were adversaries. We were together; we were alone. We were a marriage.

EIGHT

January 11, 2007

I woke up this morning and glanced at the alarm clock that tells the date as well as the time: this cold, sunny Thursday would have been our thirty-third wedding anniversary. Odd that I should remember the date's significance because I had forgotten it for most of our married life. Almost in a reversal of roles, Bruce always remembered (weren't husbands the ones who more typically forgot?) and brought me roses, engraved silver letter openers, decorative hearts of white and pink marble—hearts that would never break.

My "married life"—how odd the phrase sometimes seems—as if that portion, those years, exist only as an entity, a period of time that I sometimes think I can extrapolate from my life despite my comments to the contrary earlier in this recollection. I have to laugh to myself when I am filling out information forms and reach the question indicating my "marital status." Should I check the box "Single" since I am now alone? Should I check the box "Married" because I once was? Often, there is no option, no middle ground between the two, and so I find myself in some vague, indefinable state of existence and identity. I loath the term "widow" (redolent of long, black dresses; dried flowers; and a certain "musty-ness" of spirit, a deprivation of joy), but then what else am I? A friend who had not known Bruce said to me a few days ago that she always thinks of me as "just Barbara" because she often forgets that I was married—that I had a life with a husband—just as she does now. I have other friends tell me that they cannot conceive of their lives without their partners—and in my more bitter (jealous?) moments I mentally reply, "Well, you may damn well have to at some point."

And so here is my anger—anger at those situations, often at a dinner party, when I cease to exist as the conversation is engaged only among the couples present, anger at myself for not being bold enough to express my opinions without the support of a husband beside me, anger at myself for fearing confrontations, anger at myself for allowing some people to take advantage of my solitary state: "Let's ask Barbara; she has nothing better to do."

And so here is my anger—anger at those situations when I am not physically strong enough to put chains on the Expedition, not tall enough to reach the items on the top shelves in the local hardware store, not wise enough to acknowledge that four hours of sleep a night is not adequate, not determined enough to lose the weight I have gained, not prudent enough to stop spending money . . . .

And so here is my anger—anger at all the "shoulds" and "should nots" that people (often with the best of intentions) feel free to say to me: "You should exercise more"; "You shouldn't drive to California alone"; "You should sell (the boat, the Mustang)"; "You shouldn't buy so many (books, clothes, shoes, earrings and rings, wallets, bottles of Scotch)"; "You should eat more regularly"; "You shouldn't leave the house unlocked at night"; "You should balance your checkbook"; "You shouldn't act as if you had a twenty-five-year-old-body or a twenty-five-year-old brain"; "You should learn to say 'no'" ; "You shouldn't stay up half the night"; "You should remarry."

And so here is my anger at the parts of my marriage that I cannot fix, anger at myself for the compromises I made and am still making, anger at my fractured life, anger at my loss—anger deepening and widening to a degree best expressed by Edna St. Vincent Millay in one of the most bitter metaphors about grief I have ever read:

> *Strange how few,*
> *After all's said and done, the things that are*
> *Of moment.*
> > *Few indeed! When I can make*
> *Of ten small words a rope to hang the world!*
> *"I had you and I have you now no more."*

> *from "Interim"*

From my journal:

I tried to glue together the jade bracelet I broke when I fell up my flagstone stairs, but some things cannot be fixed. How interesting it is that inanimate objects so easily become metaphors for aspects of our lives. Bruce bought the bracelet for me in Hong Kong to celebrate my fortieth birthday—a smooth green bangle with gold clasps. Jade—considered to be lucky—and now the bracelet is broken beyond repair. Here is my life now that Bruce is dead—in pieces, the good fortune gone.

And so here is my anger—the third step in the process—so late in coming and augmenting the resentment, the pain, the bitterness I feel.

NINE

April 12, 2002

Now I am at the end, or perhaps I should say at the "true point of beginning" as the land surveyors write on their maps, at that point in time when my life was changed forever by thirty minutes—the "duration of event" (such cold words!)—on Bruce's death certificate. Thirty minutes, thirty years: what difference does it make when all is gone in an instant?

The day Bruce died should have been filled with premonitions: a sullen grey sky laden with storm clouds that hurled rain against the windows; a varied thrush on the deck below with a neck broken from hitting the glass, its body still soft and warm to the touch; the vine maples tossed by the force of the wind, some of their leaves stripped by the unseasonable weather. Death should arrive like one of the Four Horsemen in Albrecht Durer's great print of the Apocalypse—thundering across a tumultuous sky on a pale, gaunt horse and armed with bow and arrow or sword or scythe.

But no! Death came silently—unannounced, unpredicted on a day that began with complete calm and the remnants of fair weather clouds, a lovely but unremarkable spring day. I remember very little of that morning other than taking the obligatory trip to town to pick up the mail and standing in front of the post office while Bruce talked with a few friends, my thoughts drifting to how we might spend the evening with no plans on the calendar, the sun bright and warm on my hair and shoulders.

Home by noon. I arranged lettuce leaves and slices of tomatoes, cold turkey, and wheat bread on a small platter ("Oh, damn! I forgot to buy mayonnaise again."). I set the table methodically as usual: knife and spoon on the right, the solitary fork on the left, the yellow paper napkin folded into a triangle, the glass nestled above the knife and the spoon (the satisfaction of simple orderliness, I told myself—the small comforts of routine daily life). Before I had a chance to call him to lunch, Bruce came upstairs, complaining of an irregular heart rate. He went into the bedroom and about ten minutes later, he came back into the kitchen, saying nothing had changed, his voice somewhat tentative. I cannot recall those moments in the light of what was about to happen, but I said, "Let's go to the Clinic, just to be sure." He was unusually acquiescent: did he know something he refused to tell me, even then? Did he suspect the worst? Did I look at him carefully? Did I see anything amiss? I don't think so because I placed the perishables back in the refrigerator, put our dog Frosty in her crate ("Be good, pup-pup; we'll be right back."), and picked up the keys to the Expedition as if this were just another errand on the day's list. Was what I perceived as his calmness a profound, inexpressible fear? I will never know.

From my journal:

I started the car, readjusted the rear view mirror, and slowly backed up the driveway, turning the wheel sharply to avoid the grass and weed-filled ditches as I straightened out the tires onto the gravel road. Had we spoken as we left the house? Had we spoken once we were in the car? What were the last words he said to me? I wish I could remember—the silence still haunts me: what did he know? what did he feel?

As I pulled the gear shift out of reverse and into drive, Bruce slumped over with a groan like nothing I had ever heard before. I forced myself to be calm as I drove back down the driveway, thinking carefully: "Put the gearshift in park; set the emergency brake; turn off the engine." I ran down the steps to the house, slid the key into the lock, and crossed the tile entranceway, whispering to my surprised dog that "It's all right; everything is going to be all right"—the words catching in my throat as I picked up the cordless phone, dialed 911.

"What is your emergency?"

Forcing my voice to be deliberate and clear, I replied, "My husband is having a heart attack. Oh, please, please help me." I gave the dispatcher my address as completely as I could, and his questions continued as I ran back up the steps.

"Can you get him out of the car?"

"No, I can't; I can't!" (Don't you understand? Don't you realize my husband weighs 200 pounds?)

"Can you breathe for him?"

"I will try." (I don't know what to do. It's not enough; I can't breathe hard enough!)

"Can you feel a pulse?"

"No! Oh, please, please hurry!" (Oh, my God! I can't feel anything!)

I managed to recline the seat part way and push his head against the headrest. I tried to breathe for him, to fill his lungs with air. Then I looked into his eyes, and I knew that my husband, slumped backwards in the seat in front of me as I tried to maintain my balance on the running board, was dying and that there was nothing neither I nor anyone else could do to save him. How did I know? What inner voice told me even at that moment that there was absolutely no hope?

Suddenly two men were running down my driveway, pulling my husband from the car onto the ground, starting CPR. Then the ambulance, more people, the distraught faces of neighbors, some in tears. I sat on the top step of the stairs that descended to my house with one of the captains from the Fire Department, his hand on my shoulder, his hand where my husband's will never be again. I listened to what was going on behind me ("Don't look") as I grew more and more numb. Finally, one of the EMTs came over to me and gently asked if I wanted to say anything to my husband ("Hearing is the last sense to go"). I knelt down on the gravel beside Bruce's body, the rocks sharp against my knees, and against all reason, against all that my intellect told me was possible, I fervently hoped that he could hear me say, "I love you; wait for me."

Twenty agonizing minutes passed as the sheriff tried to find my home—his presence mandatory because my husband (the medical doctor) had not been in a physician's care during the past twenty-four hours. The irony of this moment would come to me later, but all I knew in that instant was that I <u>had</u> to move Bruce's body off the gravel ("I know this is hurting him") and yet I could not until the sheriff arrived. I cannot remember his questions, but I do recall the awkwardness of the ride in the ambulance to the Clinic. Through the back window I could see the sheriff following us, his lights no longer flashing ("What is the need now?"), and the absurdity of the situation as I agonized about whether one was supposed to talk to the two EMTs riding in the back of the ambulance with me and the body of my husband strapped on a gurney. If so, then about what? The weather? What had just happened? What am I supposed to do with <u>this</u> silence? Then one of the EMTs covered my hand with his, a gesture so compassionate and kind, a gesture I will remember forever.

I sat in a chair in one of the exam rooms at the Clinic, feeling very small, very pale. The room was cold and white, the lights too bright. I desperately wanted to leave; yet I answered more questions with a remarkable degree of control (I did not cry; I could not cry) until a friend arrived and took over for me. I felt myself growing even smaller, even more pale until I felt nothing at all—nothing at all, that is, until I told the mainland funeral director (undertaker? mortician? what do they call themselves these days?) that I wanted to see my husband one more time.

"He's already in the vehicle; I need to leave."

And so here is my anger: Oh, God damn you; God damn you! You can miss the ferry; you can miss every ferry for the rest of your God-damned life! Just do what I want. You <u>will</u> do what I want!

"I don't care; I <u>want</u> to see him." I tried to control my voice, but the words caught in my throat. Why was I so hoarse? Why was it so difficult suddenly to speak, to demand the one thing I wanted at that moment and was not about to lose?

"I don't care; I <u>must</u> see him. You <u>must</u> do this for me!" I finally forced the words out of my mouth, the intensity of my anger tasting like metal on my tongue.

With an air of one greatly inconvenienced, the man left, and I waited until one of the nurses returned, placing her hand on my shoulder as she led me down the hall.

I walked into the darkened exam room: the dim light that came from under the cabinets was soft and warm. Alone, I was alone in the room, this time the silence a welcome presence. I made no move to uncover Bruce's face; I touched his arm lying under the thin white cover and whispered once more, "I love you; wait for me." I stood motionless, afraid to stay but more afraid to leave—because once I let go, once I left that room, Bruce would be gone forever. When I finally was forced to admit to myself that there was no point in remaining any longer, I walked out of the exam room, the corridor lights harsh and bright in my eyes, pushed open the Clinic doors, and slipped into the warmth of that spring afternoon, the sky now filled with light grey clouds and a gentle breeze.

I have no further memories of the rest of that day other than spending the night at my neighbors' home—at their insistence, too numb to resist. Out of kindness, they gave me their bed but warned me that I might have to let in their cats sometime during the night should they scratch at the sliding glass door. Sleep was impossible so I pulled up the covers, lying on my side, looking out into the darkness, waiting for the cats to appear. An hour or so later, I saw their faces at the door and let them into the room. They jumped onto the bed with the agile, silent grace that only cats possess and looked briefly at each other and then at me ("Who is this stranger?") before curling up their soft grey and black bodies on the empty pillow next to mine, their throaty, slightly raspy purrs filling the silence until dawn.

TEN

April-May 2002

In the days that followed Bruce's death, I marked the ebb and flow of friends who spent hours around my kitchen table, talking honestly of their own sorrows, losses, personal failures, as if my grief opened a door to theirs. United by regret and sadness, we nevertheless tried to laugh at each other's frailties as we drank beer and ate pizzas well into the night, sleep no longer a priority. We talked at length about our lives during the years of Vietnam as if all of us who experienced that war to some degree or another were forever compelled to talk about that profoundly disruptive time. In a way, we were all injured—but not to the horrible degree of our friends who were able to return from Danang, Saigon—their survival compromised in ways I could never imagine. We confessed to the marijuana and the hashish we had smoked; we confessed to the chaos of our personal relationships—mine with Bruce no exception; we found comfort in the similarity of our experiences whether in Iowa City or in Berkeley or in Madison—separated by miles of distance but not of spirit. I remembered my relief that Bruce did not have to go to Vietnam, but spent his military commitment in the Army doing laser research at an aging arsenal in Philadelphia—research he hated in an environment he hated even more while I was equally miserable working for an insurance company in Hartford, writing technical manuals for computer terminal operators. However, in thinking about those two-plus years Bruce was in Philadelphia, I was able to remember with joy the first trip we took together before we were married and before he returned to the Midwest to join the practice where he would spend the next three decades of his—and then—our lives.

With little money and in an aging red and black Mercury Cougar that started only fitfully and whose dash lights failed at night, we drove up the Eastern seaboard one July to the Canadian Maritime Provinces, eating scallops and loving the mist and rain that fell upon us most of the time. In Digby Neck, Nova Scotia, we rented the last available cabin in a resort whose name I have long forgotten. Out of all the hundreds of photographs of our travels together, sadly none exist of this trip, and so I must rely solely on my memories. I recall fragments of days, the constant worry that the Cougar would not start in the mornings, the constant belief that surely it would one more time; the realization that we did not have enough money to afford motel rooms on the drive back to Philadelphia, the realization that it did not matter. In the little cabin on Digby Neck, we sat on the small front porch with our feet on the railings, talking for hours as the rain softly fell throughout the night; we listened to an old brown radio (no television, no telephones) on a ledge above the small kitchen table made of yellow formica; we soaked in a claw-footed cast iron bathtub so high above the floor that I barely could swing my legs over the side. Then we slipped into the twin beds which we pushed together so that we could hold each other as the hours passed until dawn. We were so happy those nights . . . all those nights which accumulated into the weeks, the months, the years to this point in time when I am recalling a distant past with my friends around another kitchen table.

ELEVEN

December 2002

Snow fell this morning with an unaccustomed gentleness. In Iowa, wind usually accompanied snow; here the flakes fell straight down surrounded by a silence that was almost ethereal. I walked with Frosty to the end of the road, our tracks the only imprints on the soft, white surface. The beauty of these early hours reinforced my decision to stay home for Christmas, despite entreaties from my family and friends that "I should not be alone on the holidays." Not only did I desire the solitude, but this year I wanted to be in my own home.

A number of women had told me that they had stopped decorating for the holidays once their husbands or companions were gone. This attitude seemed so self-defeating: why wouldn't you want your home full of Christmas this time of year? Why wouldn't you want to brighten your surroundings with evergreen garlands, bowls of fragrant potpourri, strings of cranberries for the tree?

Oh, yes, the tree. For a number of years, I had decorated a small artificial spruce with bird ornaments of every kind imaginable. White bird lights flew through the limbs that were covered with other birds of wood, porcelain, and glass. I had stitched a chickadee, a blue bird, a cardinal; a woodpecker in black, red and white wool hung from top next to a yellow-feathered parakeet.

However, this year I needed something new. I had found a large madrona limb on the road one morning after a storm and had dragged it home, anticipating some future, undefined use. Here was my tree! I proceeded to spray it with gold paint and wedged it into my old Christmas tree stand. I covered the limbs with gold ornaments and gold tinsel and draped my favorite tree skirt around the base—a round of black fabric covered with white doves carrying branches laden with red berries. I placed all my teddy bears on a doll's sled on the dining room table, along with sparkling reindeer and fragrant candles. Finally, I hung our stockings on the mantel: Frosty's with an appliqued dog biscuit, mine with "Barbara" in velvet script, and the large needlepoint I had made for Bruce over 15 years ago of Santa about to descend a chimney with his bulging sack of presents.

When I was finished, I started the logs in the fireplace burning with a minimal amount of effort (Bruce would have been proud) and sat with Frosty by the hearth, looking at my living room with some degree of satisfaction and determined to push away any feelings of loneliness and sadness. Yet in spite of all my efforts at decorating, something was missing. As I continued to look around the room, I realized that there were no presents under the tree. I smiled to myself as I thought of how Bruce would come home with an abundance of shopping bags and disappear after requesting wrapping paper, scissors, and tape—only to reappear hours later carrying boxes covered with tissue and shining ribbons—boxes that had to be opened in a certain order, saving the best for last. I often wondered if his generosity at Christmas was a reaction against all those empty Christmases he had endured as a child. He desired no gifts himself but gave abundantly to all those about whom he cared.

As I looked at my little gold tree bereft of gifts, my thoughts drifted back through the months to the time following Bruce's death. On Memorial Day, I had placed evergreens and flowers on the driveway where I had knelt beside my husband for the last time; I had watched the morning fog slowly dissipate as the light increased from the east; I had noticed that the sunlight lingered later and later as the days moved toward the summer solstice. A solitary bald eagle had soared past my windows, only to return to the limb of a Douglas-fir where the magnificent bird had remained far longer than was typical—a vision that was repeated every April to follow—the eagles reassuring simply by their presence and providing a meaning or a message in a universe that is beyond my understanding.

As the logs diminished and the coals glowed a deeper red, casting flickering shadows on my walls, I remembered how my friends had brought Bruce's ashes to me in a beautifully hand-crafted box made of yellow heart and purple heart—his two favorite woods; how my friends had brought yellow tulips, cards, books; how my friends had brought compassion, understanding, and love. Here was the enduring good that had come from Bruce's death: I had gained the awareness that there are people in this world who exemplify a compassion and an understanding so extraordinary that I have no words to describe how their presence in my life makes me feel.

From the fifteen or so "angels" who had tried to save my husband's life, to the friends and relatives who had spent hours with me during those first few devastating weeks, to the Episcopal priest whose forthright words and intuitive awareness of what I needed had given me great solace, to the patients who had sent cards that bespoke sorrow and consolation—I knew these people truly embodied what the poet Mary Oliver called the "unspeakable kindness" of the world.

As I closed the fireplace doors and walked Frosty one more time before bed, I realized what I had been given in those months was a timeless gift that could not be wrapped in shining paper and placed under any tree, but rather was a recognition that transcended death and allowed me to believe once again that the world could be as gentle and spiritual as the lightly falling snow.

TWELVE

In the spring of 2004, I flew to Namibia to join friends from California at the lodge of a European couple Bruce and I had met years earlier on one of our first journeys to Africa. The prior November I had traveled to Mexico, in no small part to see whether I could function with some degree of confidence in a group of strangers once again, account for my single state with minimal explanation, and find the renewal that Bruce and I always had discovered while visiting a new country. What I gained most from that trip to Mexico was an awareness that could never be captured through the lens of a camera but rather was brought into sharp focus by the nightmare of a fellow traveler's almost incomprehensible loss: a husband dead from a heart attack and two young sons killed in a single-car accident within a three-month period. How she continued to live—to even <u>want</u> to live—was an example of courage that I will always remember—an awareness in which I recognized the capacity of human beings to embrace life, to hold it with all their strength in the face of the reality stated in the Episcopalian service for the Burial of the Dead: "In the midst of life we are in death." However true those words are, we still think of existence, not its opposite. And so I found I could return to Namibia the following year without fear and with a purpose: to leave a part of what I had so dearly loved behind in this most fitting of places: Africa—the land that kept calling us back year after year, the land that held memories deep in our hearts.

May 2004

On the flight from Amsterdam to Johannesburg, I thought of the troubled continent below me that was plagued with pointless and seemingly endless wars; the countries that were ruined by famine, AIDS, greed, too many people; the contempt of Whites for Blacks that I saw in the eyes of a white woman for the Blacks who worked for her at her fishing camp in

Zambia—a litany of problems that appeared unsolvable. However, when I looked out the window of the plane, I saw the beauty of a spectacular sunset. The sky was streaked with red, orange, and deep purple clouds that stretched across the entire horizon, and I found myself remembering other African sunsets that Bruce and I had seen together. I thought of the enormous red disk of the sun as it sank into the waters of Lake Kariba; I thought of the late soft light illuminating the lionesses on the banks of the South Luanga River while a small herd of elephants crossed the river further downstream; I thought of the anticipation of what we might see in the darkness of the night drives—the eyes of prey and hunter alike glowing in the surrounding blackness, the impossible wealth of the stars covering the sky. Coming full circle, I remembered the time just before dawn when sight gave way to the senses of touch and sound: the chill, damp early morning air; the warmth of a cup of coffee; the songs of the Cape Turtle doves; the laughter of the guides as they loaded the vehicles for another game drive, the chatter of the troups of baboons. Then sight regained ascendancy as the sun started to rise, brightening the sky as the stars grew more and more pale, eventually fading away.

The following morning I flew to Windhoek and then boarded a small charter plane that would take me to Huab Lodge where I would meet my companions. The pilot was stocky, with a ruddy face, blond hair, and hands covered with freckles. I noticed the gold band he was wearing and tried to imagine what his wife was like and whether she was content with her supremely confidant, perhaps arrogant, young husband. I had a brief moment of longing to be a girl, young and in love, and not this older woman who was tired and traveling alone and trying to find some purpose to her life.

However, my sad thoughts drifted away as I looked at the landscape below: the dry plains crossed by few roads; the enormous upheavals of the land, twisted and scarred and stratified with layers of orange and tan and black; the flamingoes rising in a single mass of pink and white from a large, brackish lagoon; the streaks of falling rain that never reached the ground. We flew over the enormous Cape Fur seal colony on the coast where I had taken one of my favorite photographs of my husband sitting among the rocks, surrounded by a multitude of sleek grey bodies, flippers, and whiskered noses, and looking over his shoulder at me with a smile of disbelief on his face that he should find himself in this position.

Finally, the familiar sights of Huab Lodge came into view: the thatched roof of the large lodge that served as cocktail lounge and dining area; the line of smaller, individual rooms with white-washed walls and thatched roofs similar to that of the lodge, ascending the hill to the solar panels that the baboons periodically stole and then just as inexplicably returned. I tried not to cry as the plane touched down on the small dirt runway, and I saw the owners and my friends standing by one of the pale yellow Land Rovers, waiting in anticipation for me.

Huab Lodge

Just before sunrise one morning, my friends and I, along with the owner of the Lodge and two exuberant black Labrador retrievers, walked down the dusty Huab River bed and climbed Cannon Hill—a rocky formation of pale yellow boulders; shepherd's trees; and brittle, dry grasses that began to glow as the promise of the rising sun grew brighter in the east, the long, thin clouds streaked with deep red and purple that started to fade as the sun began to appear over the distant mountaintops.

As we reached the crest of the hill, the dogs grew strangely silent, lying on the boulders near my friend Jan's feet, their heads between their front paws. We stood for a moment in awkward silence until Jan started to speak—the sun now above the mountains, the dry grasses backlit to a pure white. "Here is where I want to be buried, also, but for now it will be Bruce who will witness the sunrises, watch the seasons come and go, and be the first to see the Huab River run full of water once more."

My friends recited humorous verses that Bruce had so enjoyed and read "In Blackwater Woods," Mary Oliver's simple but profound meditation about how to live in this world and how to accept death when it inevitably comes:

> To live in this world
> you must be able
> to do three things:
> to love what is mortal;
> to hold it
> against your bones knowing

your own life depends on it;
and, when the time comes to let it go,
to let it go.

In a surprisingly steady voice, I read the last lines from Pablo Neruda's poignant poem "The Watersong Ends" as the sun climbed higher in the African sky, its warmth a benediction, a moment of grace bestowed upon us all.

For my part and yours, we comply, we share our hopes and
  winters;
and we have been wounded not only by mortal enemies
but by mortal friends (that seemed all the more bitter),
but bread does not seem to taste sweeter, nor my book, in the
  meantime—
living, we supply the statistics that pain still lacks,
we go on loving love and in our blunt way
we bury the liars and live among the truth-tellers.

My love, night came down, galloping over the spread of the
  world.
My love, night erases all trace of the sea, the ship heels, is at
  rest.
My love, night lit up its starry institution.

To the place by the sleeping man, the woman glided in her
  wakefulness
and in dreams the two descended the rivers which led to the
  weeping
and grew once again among dark animals and trains loaded with
  shadows
to the point of being nothing more than pale stones at night.

It is time, love, to break off that sombre rose,
shut up the stars and bury the ash in the earth;
and in the rising of the light, wake with those who awoke
or go on in the dream, reaching the other shore of the sea
  which has no other shore.

From the brown and orange earthenware jar Jan and his wife Suzi had given me, I scattered my husband's ashes on the ground and over the grasses as I struggled futilely with the tears I had managed to suppress in order to read these words. We stood a few more moments in silence and then, reluctantly, and with our hands on each other's shoulders, we slowly walked down the hill, preceded by the dogs who started cavorting and running with abandon down the river bed only when their human companions were back on level ground.

The following morning I returned to the top of Cannon Hill, accompanied only by the dogs that, once more, sat with absolute stillness while I watched the sunrise. My friends told me later that when they went to the Hill without me on the third day, the dogs were no longer quiet but exuberant with joy and the expectation of abundant sticks to chase. What did the dogs know, what did they sense, in their canine wisdom? What made those first two mornings different from the third? I cannot explain this, nor do I want to, because much of life should remain a mystery, not open for dissection or rational explanation. And it was at that moment and for the first time since Bruce died that I felt a sense of life having come full circle to its inevitable conclusion—a conclusion not to be feared or mourned but accepted for what it was.

Later that day, I went to the hot springs, removed all of my clothes, and slipped into the shallow warm water that soothed and comforted me, falling into a deep, untroubled sleep. When I awoke, I looked up at the same clear blue sky that Beryl Markham had seen as she flew over Africa, heading west with the night to another continent, on the far side of which was my home, my life yet to live.

THIRTEEN

Spring 2007

Early one morning, knowing what I now had to do, I sought out my "secret spot" beneath the heavy red limbs of the madrona tree near the cliff's edge in front of our home, the rain falling softly through the deep green leaves. To the casual onlooker, I must have appeared mad—this woman stumbling over the rocks with her disheveled hair, the hem of her white chenille robe covered with seeds and twigs, her slippers dark and wet. I gently scattered the remainder of my husband's ashes that mingled with the moss, the earth, the stones of this ancient mountain top upon which I live. And so here it is that I, too, have come to rest, the place he brought me to before he died. As I write these last lines, I see Bruce standing by the door, about to leave and looking over his shoulder at me as he so often did, fastening the clasps with ease on the heavy Italian gold bracelet that I now wear, smiling and telling me, "Let gravity do the work for you." And so here it is that my heart, my soul have become deeply anchored in the granite that ties my home to the ground, a gravity of spirit and love that will keep me here for the years I have left to live. As I write these last lines, the full moon is setting in the west with the night, its golden light shining down the smooth water and through the evergreens that hold the promise of the peace I will someday feel.

www.ingramcontent.com/pod-product-compliance
Lightning Source LLC
Chambersburg PA
CBHW061225280526
45784CB00006B/2630